MAKING

YOUR

GOALS

A

REALITY

MAKING

YOUR

GOALS

A

REALITY

BY LEGENDARY CELEBRITY PSYCHIC
KENNY KINGSTON

AS TOLD TO VALERIE PORTER

SEVEN LOCKS PRESS

Santa Ana, California
Minneapolis, Minnesota
Washington, D.C.

Seven Locks Press
P.O. Box 25689
Santa Ana, CA 92799
(800) 354-5348

Individual Sales. This book is available through most bookstores or can
be ordered directly from Seven Locks Press at the address above.

Quantity Sales. Special discounts are available on quantity purchases by
corporations, associations, and others. For details, contact the "Special
Sales Department" at the publisher's address above.

Printed in the United States of America

Library of Congress Cataloging-in-Publication Data
is available from the publisher
ISBN 0-929765-21-4

Cover and Interior Design by Sparrow Advertising & Design

To all of my Sweet Spirits who've made the transition to the other side. I'm grateful for their presence and for their loving assistance in giving me these glorious affirmations to help and comfort you as long as you spend time on this place called Earth.

And to your beloved ones who are *your* Sweet Spirits, guiding and protecting you each day of your life.

Introduction

RELAX, RELEASE, AND REACH OUT TO THE GOOD AROUND YOU

The more relaxed you are—the more content and confident you feel—the better you'll be able to open up to the spiritual universe and all the wonderful things it has to offer you.

Are you searching for greater happiness but feel it's eluded you? Or perhaps you feel your life is going quite well but you'd like to enhance what you already have by attaining even greater happiness and success.

There are techniques I recommend that can offer you the comfort, guidance, and additional strength you deserve. They can help you not only fully enjoy the life you already have, but also help you reach for *and accomplish* your higher goals.

Now, we're going to focus on developing an even better and happier *inner you*—this is the key. When you feel good about YOU, you fear not the world.

The first step toward making your dreams come true and achieving what you want in life is to not avoid facing those dreams and goals head-on. Why keep them tucked away in a secret corner of your mind, hoping that one day something will happen? That day may never arrive, unless you take an active part in MAKING it happen! So many times people will say, "Oh, sure, I'd like to go to Europe *some day* . . . but I can't afford it right now." But wait! Those same people may have taken two or three short trips during the course of a year—a few days gambling in Las Vegas or Atlantic City, a long weekend in the mountains, a week by the ocean or lake. Count up the expenses of those short trips, and you'd probably find that the trip to Europe might not have cost much more (particularly if your luck is less than perfect in Las Vegas or Atlantic City!). Rather than dreaming about that European vacation, make it a priority and make it your reality!

So many times I've had clients tell me, "My sister is ill and I really should go to visit her, but I can't take the time off work right now." Yet, sadly, somehow, if the sister passes away, the person makes the time to go to the funeral or memorial service. Why not put that same time and effort into visiting someone while he or she is still on Earthplane? My motto has always been, "Only Believe; All Things Are Possible If You Only Believe." There IS a way to make things work, Sweet Spirits. It IS within your power. Eliminate such phrases as "I'm too old," "I'm not brave enough," "I just can't do that." Give yourself more power than that. YOU CAN DO IT!

Naturally, this book has a specific and all-important purpose, which is to help you make your goals a reality. Whether or not you're deeply involved in the psychic or spiritual world, I know you can benefit from these pages.

Just in case you're not familiar with the beautiful world of spirit, there are a few terms which I feel I should explain so that you can obtain the maximum benefit from the book. Those terms will be explained at the end of this section. Keep in mind that whether or not you're fully indoctrinated into the psychic field and whether or not you're 100 percent a believer in all aspects of psychic phenomena, there are benefits to be obtained from this book.

And of course, regardless of your faith or religion, it's possible to believe in the spiritual concepts I'm about to relay. All religions are accepted by the spirit realm. This book is not about religion. I believe God (or whatever powerful force you believe in) is everywhere, whether you go to a particular church or not.

In our brief time together on the following pages, I will help you unlock the strength and happiness within you, using my ideas for meditation and visualization techniques as well as affirmations that can be applied to any number of situations you may face. Let's begin!

DEFINING SOME IMPORTANT TERMS

Guardian angel/higher force/spirit guide

Many people recall hearing a relative telling them they had a "guardian angel"—someone very special watching over and protecting them. It's a wonderfully comforting thought, and I take exception with only one aspect: A guardian angel needn't be an untouchable, remote "being." Our loved ones in spirit can be our guardian angels. The term "spirit guide" is interchangeable with guardian angel, for a spirit guide's mission is to aid, comfort, and guide us. And a "higher force" is also a guiding force in spirit, though in most cases, it refers to a highly-elevated or advanced spirit, even a deity or religious figure.

Medium

You may need to read some of the explanations below before understanding this particular category. The term "medium" refers to someone who receives information from the spirit world. Mediums communicate with spirits of your loved ones, who give them information and guidance to help you. The true purpose and ultimate goal of a medium, in my opinion, is not just to make contact with a spirit (which of course is important in itself). This is really only the beginning. The ultimate goal is for the medium to make contact with the spirit and then interpret the message the spirit provides, which will give real, applicable advice to someone about his or her past, present and future.

Other Side

This is also referred to as the "spirit world" and is the realm where we exist when we pass away. This is not a *place* so much as an energy force or level of vibration. It's called the "other side" in order to depict just how close spirits are to us (as though on the other side of the street, the other side of a bridge, etc.). We who believe in *spiritualism* (see below) feel that our loved ones and friends are only in the next room, so to speak. They are within our reach and can be around us when we need them.

Psychic

A psychic is someone who offers guidance and advice about one's past, present and future. Psychics are NOT to be confused with magicians and they are not reading your mind. To give psychic readings, they may use many tools, such as tarot cards, crystal balls, psychometry (touching an object which has been close to a person and picking up psychic messages from it) or clairaudio (listening to the sound of a voice and receiving psychic vibrations from it). Not all psychics are, by any means, mediums.

For those who may not know, I am a psychic/medium, which means I have the best of both worlds. I am a psychic, which means I tell clients who come to me for private sessions about their past, present and future, and I receive this information by contacting the spirit world. I also apply these gifts (and to me they are true gifts) when roaming through the audience giving brief messages during lecture appearances or anytime when I encounter a spirit around someone.

Spiritualism

For some, this is a form of religion. For others, it's less a religion and more a powerful belief. Spiritualism refers to the idea that when we pass away, we do not "die," but rather we take on a spirit form. It is the belief that while we may be composed of body and soul while alive, the soul transcends the passing and survives.

Trial period

This is a term I use to refer to a time of our lives when things appear to be extremely difficult and appear to be going entirely wrong. My belief is that this may be happening *intentionally*. Our guide, or a higher force, may be testing our strength and our desire to achieve something, so that we will truly appreciate the good when it arrives.

Trial periods *do* make us stronger. They build character. Oftentimes a trial period better equips us to handle problems (or avoid them) in the future.

GOALS

Goals and ambitions are wonderful. They give us a reason for living, a reason for getting up in the morning, if you will. But as I always tell people, AIM HIGH. Dare to dream of the best possible scenario, the best possible life you can imagine for yourself, then reward yourself every step of the way. If your dream is to become a bank president, it might not happen immediately. But if you are hired by a bank in some capacity, congratulate yourself! You're one step closer to achieving your goal. Be the best you can be at whatever you're doing at the moment. You are starting on your highway to success.

And as I often tell my private clients, don't rest until you've gone to the person with the highest level of authority—the one whom you feel is the most appropriate person to help you in a particular situation. In the military, it's mandatory to follow the chain of command in terms of contacting certain people and making requests. But in our daily lives, there needn't be such a chain of command. Use your freedom of choice and GO DIRECTLY TO THE GENERAL (the "General" being the person whom you feel is truly "in charge" of the situation) for the answer you need. Then, once you feel you've succeeded in contacting that person, you can know in your heart that you've taken a step toward making something happen. Even if you get an answer of "no" from that particular person, you can take pride in knowing you did your best, and you can then move on, finding another way to achieve your goal or perhaps revising it slightly.

Remember: Never underestimate the importance of goals. They give you drive, dedication, and determination, and often lead to success. Goals are a secret desire burning within you. But rather than *keeping* them secret, why not write those goals down, so that you can look at them from time to time? The subconscious mind is a powerful tool—just seeing your goals in print can help you visualize them and believe they're already a reality.

I've provided you with some blank pages where you can write your goals within this book. I have also provided space where you can write goals you've already achieved along the way.

Whether your goals are major or minor, they're important to you. Write them down and always keep them close to you as a daily visual reminder. You might want to keep your long-range goals separate from your short-term ones. Short-term goals might be similar to a to-do list of steps that will help you accomplish your long-range goals. Tape one or both lists of goals inside a kitchen cupboard, medicine cabinet, or a closet door, for example—somewhere you're sure to look at least once a day. Don't be surprised if one day, as you look at what you've written, an idea springs into your mind as to how you can achieve the goal. (Perhaps you'll remember the name of a person you can call who might help you.) Jot the thought down right then and there, next to your goal, so that you won't forget to follow through. With all of the activities going on in your world, don't trust anything this important to memory.

Colors play a major role in sending out signals. I suggest writing your goals with a red felt pen if you need to recharge your energy forces, or a green felt pen for an improvement in financial conditions. Since green is also a symbol of healing, it can be used to send out the vibrations for improvement in health for yourself or a loved one.

As you accomplish a short-range goal, know that it is bringing you a step closer to achieving what you desire (even if it's a package mailed or a phone call made). Do not underestimate any of these accomplishments, no matter how minor they may seem to you. Count each step along the way as an achievement, a personal blessing. Look at the secret place where you keep your written goals. Then, physically take a pen and *cross off* that step or "mini goal." This tells you that you've achieved what you set out to do and you're ready to take the next step and move on. Your list then becomes not only a list of goals but a success chart, as well. Your long-range goal is then closer at hand.

Several female clients of mine keep a daily list of their goals in their purse. They say it helps give them energy as they move through their day. If this works for you, carry your goals with you. Keep them close to your mind and heart, body and soul.

You might want to write your goals in a notebook and leave it open on your desk at home or at work. Or you might write a particularly important goal on a piece of paper and keep it in a different location from the others, to stress its importance. Use whatever method works best for you.

⫸GOALS FOR TODAY⫷

⟶GOALS FOR TODAY⟵

—GOALS FOR THIS WEEK—

─GOALS FOR THIS WEEK─

DAILY MEDITATIONS

The visual act of writing goals is a powerful beginning. In addition to this, it's possible to verbalize certain phrases each day to get the most *from* that day.

May I suggest the following phrases as your mottos—your attitudes—for each day of the week. Start the day by reading the corresponding phrases, to put yourself in the proper frame of mind for what lies ahead:

MONDAY

"I overcome any excesses of the weekend, and any fears of the week ahead. I am not feeling sorry that my weekend of relaxation is over, but I keep that relaxed feeling with me today. I have energy and enthusiasm and I feel so rested from the weekend. I look forward to the week ahead and all that can be accomplished. I am optimistic and strong. I use my energy to begin new projects. I feel and I know that I am ready to become a better person."

TUESDAY

"I call upon the Master and the higher forces to help me continue putting new ideas into action. I have no tension or anxiety as my responsibilities or projects grow; I am confident and capable. I am still optimistic, still strong."

WEDNESDAY

"As the middle of the work week approaches, I will finish as many projects as I can. I will also begin new projects to replace the old, and will feel confident that I will complete them, as well, in their due time. I truly expand my horizons and I see prosperity all around me. I stay in touch with my needs and know I can attract success. I refuse to accept discouragement if something is not turning out quite as I expected, or is not being completed as I had wanted. Discouragement is not part of my vocabulary. I realize that the timing may simply be off slightly, and that there may be a reason I haven't attained something yet. I will rest if my energy slips a bit. I know that I don't have to wait for the weekend to relax my mind and body. I deserve the luxury of a brief but necessary break at any time."

THURSDAY

"I let go of past limitations or restrictions that may have held me back. If something has not been accomplished, I do not feel panic because the work week is nearly over. I remember that there is a reason for everything, so perhaps some of the things I wanted or directions I'd planned to take have turned out differently for my best interest. Under no circumstances will I give up. I will continue working and give it my best efforts, yet I will begin to release any stress from the work week."

FRIDAY

"I recognize my needs and my strengths as well as my shortcomings. I cooperate with my guides and higher forces to overcome any problems and to awaken my creativity and sensitivity. I remember that I must not focus on what I *haven't* done or *haven't* received. I will reward myself for jobs well done and look forward to relaxation and the recharging of my battery, which will come with the weekend."

SATURDAY

"I dream, I dare, I do. I ease into the weekend with plenty of time for myself, daring to dream of my wildest desires and make plans to achieve them. I am pleased with my past accomplishments and eager to recharge and refresh. I will make time for my family and friends."

SUNDAY

"I pray, I believe. I give thanks for the abundance of my blessings and believe I will receive even more. I continue to rest and relax, but also make plans for a new week. I have a chance to begin again. I will aim high, but make my goals realistic."

Although I've more or less set aside Saturday and Sunday as rest days for the purposes of these meditations, I realize that many people work on a Saturday or Sunday. If you are one of those people, you might want to make up your own schedule of meditations; in other words, repeat the Saturday and Sunday meditations on those days which *are* your days off.

Realize, too, Sweet Spirits, that there is nothing wrong in working on the weekend, even if it is considered your "time off," if you are working toward achieving an all-important goal, and if the work gives you satisfaction and leads toward your being better able to relax, knowing you've achieved something.

May I also suggest, in addition to these very specific daily affirmative sayings, that you do as I do: Every morning of your life, as soon as you open your eyes and are still lying in bed, say, "Thank you, Master, for giving me another day." Remember, you're ahead. Many people do *not* see the dawning of a new day. This is a perfect way to begin each day, feeling you've been given the gift of life all over again.

AFFIRMATIONS

In addition to the positive approaches and phrases to help enhance each day, there are also phrases you can repeat at any time to help turn a negative emotion or feeling into a positive one. This is done by using affirmations, which as you may know are positive sayings that can be repeated at any time of the day or night.

My clients and friends have often asked me for special affirmations to use for important times in their lives, whether they are happy, sad, or anxious times. I've asked Spirit for help and the following are those affirmations, listed by the special need or situation. I continue to use them myself, and believe me, Sweet Spirits, they can and *do* work miracles, if you permit them to.

Use the affirmations whenever you'd like and remember that the key is to truly believe with all your heart the words you're saying. There's much more to affirmations than simply repeating words. As you say an affirmation, feel the power within you; know in your *secret* heart that you are making your dreams become a reality. Visualize yourself already claiming what you desire, be it health, happiness, or success.

But of course you must take an active part in achieving your goals. This means that, as powerful as affirmations are, you must go *beyond* them. Are you saying affirmations for good health? Then by all means make sure you're following good principles of diet, nutrition, and exercise to back up those affirmations and put them into motion.

Is peace of mind your goal? Or do you want to have a more peaceful relationship with family or friends? You'll certainly find affirmations to accommodate your needs. But here's an added bit of advice: After repeating those affirmations, try setting aside more leisure time to spend with your loved ones. Or tell that special someone that you want to work harder at achieving a happy relationship with them.

In other words, accompany your affirmations with strong, affirmative *action.* Then you'll know that you're making every possible effort toward achieving your goals, and you can expect to receive wonderful things in return.

To begin, find the category that best describes your particular situation at the moment. I've offered some thoughts on each situation—philosophy I might share with you if you were in person with me for a private psychic counseling session. If you aren't sure what category is appropriate, use the broadest context to describe your situation. In some cases, more than one category may apply and you can certainly look at affirmations in more than one category. Then, look down the list of affirmations and repeat each one. Some will "feel" better to you than others. Find the ones that seem more personally effective for you, the ones that feel "right." In many cases, you'll find that one affirmation can be used for several purposes. Some affirmations will become favorites of yours, so much so that you'll want to say them whether or not you have a particular problem. They just make you feel good about yourself! I've given you a special area at the end of this book where you can write these most treasured affirmations.

As you become more in tune, you may feel like creating your own affirmations, applying the basic tools used in the sayings I suggest. There are no rules; do what works for you. But remember, Sweet Spirits, that this is a very positive approach you're taking. Your attitude should not be, "I'll try this once and maybe it will work if it's meant to be." Instead, think not in terms of *if* but in *when* something will occur for you.

Now, here's food for thought. Is there a 100 per cent guarantee that you will achieve exactly what you desire if you follow these guidelines? Dear Sweet Spirits, no! You may not receive what you desire in exactly the way you desire it, and there may well be a good reason for that. Remember, there's always a higher force at work, a force that knows what's truly best for you. We *think* we know what's best because it's what we *want*. But what we want and what we need—for our overall spiritual, physical and emotional good—are at times two separate issues.

This higher force could certainly be of a religious nature, be it God or a Hindu deity - whomever you believe in. But it could also be a loved one of yours in spirit—your spirit guide or guardian angel—who is on the other side and in a much better position to see the bigger picture and to see what's truly going to be in your best interest.

And of course, it's always appropriate to give praise or thanks to whatever higher force helped you achieve something, whether you choose to attribute the help to an angel or spirit guide, to God or another religious being, or perhaps to a loved one in spirit whose presence you felt while repeating your affirmations.

Remember that it's easy to ask for help, but it's equally important to let those we asked know how grateful we are when the results have been achieved.

—GOALS I'VE REACHED SO FAR—

⫘GOALS I'VE REACHED SO FAR⫘

ANGER (see also FORGIVENESS)

We often think of anger as an emotional weapon we can use against someone or something else. For example, many people get into their cars and seem to feel another world war has broken out; it's a time for taking out aggression. But a car is not a weapon. With so many people using the roadways today, it seems there's enough to do just paying attention to signs and finding our way around. When you're stuck in traffic, why not use the time in your car to unwind and to look at your surroundings? You're sure to find something amusing or interesting about the world around you.

If anything, the anger you're using as a "weapon" is turning itself toward YOU: raising your blood pressure or giving you a tension headache. That certainly wasn't the intention you had, but it's the outcome, nevertheless. Is anger really worth it? Aren't you and your physical well-being more important than that?

If your response is, "Yes, my well-being *is* more important than my anger," then the power to ease your anger is within you. If you've had an argument with a friend or loved one and you're holding on to the anger, reliving the argument over and over, why not take the first step toward reconciliation? *Someone* has to pick up the phone or stop by the other person's home for a chat. Why not let that someone be you? You needn't accept the full blame for the problem, but how rewarding it could be to simply say, "I value our relationship. If you agree, let's try to work this out together."

Affirmations

1) *"I forgive and forget all that has harmed me. I am set free."*

2) *"Nothing and no one can disturb me. I can rise above any annoyances."*

3) *"I hold no grudges; my anger dissolves. I relax, release, and let go."*

4) *"My mind is gentle and harmonious."*

CONFIDENCE

There are many memorable quotes by the talented and witty British writer Oscar Wilde. My possible favorite comes from a statement he supposedly made while going through customs during some of his travels. When asked what he had to declare, Wilde responded: "I have nothing to declare except my genius."

Conceited? Some may think so. Confident? Undoubtedly so. And there *is* a difference between confidence and conceit. Having *confidence* means having trust or faith in someone or something, and certainly having confidence in ourselves should be high on the list. There's nothing wrong with believing in ourselves and having faith in our abilities or our strong points.

On the other hand, *conceit* involves having *too* high an opinion of one's self—an overexaggerated idea about our good points. On the surface, this may seem like a fine line of difference, but I'll let you in on a secret: I'd rather see you err on the side of too much confidence than not enough! Leave condemnation of yourself to someone else! Enough people will attempt, during your lifetime, to condemn you or put you down. It's inevitable that we come across people who do this in an effort to make themselves seem more important. Use your energies to love and approve of yourself, congratulate yourself for a job well done, and silently praise your best features or efforts.

Everyone has good traits, whether they're physical, scholastic, emotional, or spiritual. Play up your best features or traits. If you were blessed with attractive eyes, for example, do all you can to draw attention to them by choosing the right haircut or make-up, instead of spending all your time trying to camouflage what you interpret to be a "bad" feature, such as a couple of pounds of extra weight.

If you were given a gift of musical ability, apply that ability. Join a music appreciation class or an orchestra in your area, if possible.

In time, if you haven't already, you'll learn to walk that fine line between confidence and conceit, aware that a *quiet confidence*—knowing in your heart that you trust in yourself and your abilities, without feeling the need to shout it to the world—is perhaps one of the most delicate balances to attain, but all the more elegant and effective when it has been achieved.

Affirmations

1) *"I am perfect, whole and complete. I love and approve of myself. I am free to be me."*

2) *"I am a worthwhile person. I deserve all the good I receive."*

3) *"I am strong, secure, and confident. I face life unafraid."*

4) *"I create my own environment when I start to control my thoughts."*

5) *"Health, happiness, and prosperity are meant for me. I reach out and claim them as mine."*

6) *"I accomplish all that I set out to do."*

7) *"I rejoice in my perfection. I have no room for fear or doubt."*

COURAGE (also see FEAR)

Lack of courage, about anything from taking a test, asking for a raise, or simply getting out of bed and facing the day, can easily take root and cause us to miss out on many wonderful things in life.

Having courage doesn't mean becoming or appearing "tough" if in fact you're a very gentle person at heart. But in my opinion, true gentleness is sadly mistaken too often as a sign of weakness. Therefore it's necessary to have the courage of our own convictions—to become Master or Mistress of all we survey—calmly but definitely stating our opinions or needs without demanding.

Sometimes having the courage to be different is a difficult task. It's trendy today to carry bottled water with you, even if you're going on only a brief trip to run an errand. But if you feel uncomfortable carrying water with you (if you don't feel it's necessary or if drinking too much water doesn't seem to agree with you physically) be brave enough, courageous enough, to turn your back on trendiness and be yourself. Instead of wearing a particular fashion because it's "current," wear what suits and complements you. Wear your clothes, don't let your clothes wear you! And need I say that this also applies to harmful habits such as smoking, excessive drinking or taking drugs?

Above all, be an individual, not a copycat. Be the real you. Pretending to be something you're not takes too much energy. It's ok to be you—in fact, it's *better* than ok! If you lose a friend along the way because you won't conform to the trend or habit of the moment, consider yourself fortunate. The person who can't accept you for yourself was not your true friend to begin with.

Be brave, be quietly strong, be courageous in your own way, and be ready to reap the rewards you will receive in return.

Affirmations

1) *"There is a living force of strength within me."*

2) *"Each day I prepare for a better tomorrow."*

3) *"I make clear decisions. I am being guided properly."*

4) *"I rejoice in my perfection. I have no room for fear or doubt."*

DEPRESSION

I tell my clients that "depression is a luxury very few can afford." Please stop for a moment and read that quote again.

It's so true, isn't it? When you spend time wallowing in unhappiness, feeling sorry for yourself, it can easily become a pattern, a habit that's difficult to break.

But we are all blessed with free will. We have the choice to be happy or sad, so why be sad? There's something good to be found in every day. *Seek* happiness and you'll soon find it.

Some people feel depressed because they don't have everything they want in life—perhaps optimum health, fantastic success, or unconditional and passionate love. But, as difficult as it may be to accept this fact, I firmly believe that if we had everything we wanted, all at once, we'd soon be bored. We'd have no purpose, no drive. We'd no longer have anything to strive for or anything to look forward to.

If you haven't accomplished everything you wanted to do, reward yourself for every small achievement you *have* made. Each step is worthwhile. And, dear Sweet Spirits, don't always blame yourself if things go wrong!

Oftentimes people feel depressed without knowing what's causing it. It could be something as simple as a blood sugar problem—low blood sugar could be causing some lack of energy or enthusiasm. Try taking a piece of fruit or cheese and see if your outlook changes.

Let go of whatever may have happened in your past which you feel may be causing you to be depressed now. "The past is the past and the charm of the past is that it *is* the past" is a favorite saying of mine. Look ahead to each new day instead. Every day is a clean slate, a fresh start.

And please, stop taking each day for granted. See each day not as a burden or a punishment, but instead as a gift, a reward.

Are you still having trouble eliminating depression? Try this: *pretend* to be happy. Do your best imitation of a happy person. You'll be putting forth happy vibrations and before you know it, you may find that you're actually believing the happiness with all your heart. You'll start to feel very comfortable and natural with happiness, and the people around you will notice the difference and respond to you in a more positive way, as well. Remember that you attract what you put forward. Happy people will attract happy people. If you're depressed or lack enthusiasm, you will unfortunately attract similar people.

Affirmations:

1) *"I refuse to accept a negative thought—it doesn't belong to me."*

2) *"Health, happiness and prosperity are meant for me. I reach out and claim them as mine."*

3) *"Love surrounds and protects me. I have a special place in the Universe."*

4) *"I am filled with the pure light of love."*

5) *"Each day I prepare for a better tomorrow."*

6) *"I savor the beauty around me. I find joy in simple things."*

7) *"I am surrounded by sparkling treasures, divine gifts, exciting opportunities."*

FEAR (see also COURAGE)

You fear going to a party because you won't know anyone there.

You fear taking the exam you've been studying for.

You fear asking for a raise at work, or leaving your present job for a new opportunity you've heard about.

So many times we fear things that never happen. We take things way too seriously at times, creating monumental problems out of what, in reality, are minor concerns. We create a negative outcome to a situation that will never take place.

Suppose you go to the party you're dreading and instead of feeling all alone, you run into an old friend you haven't seen in a long time, or you make a new friend.

If you've been studying for a test, assume you'll pass it, which can occur just as easily as failing the exam.

You'll never know whether you'll get the raise unless you ask. You'll never know whether a new opportunity will work out for you unless you take the initiative to move on, leaving your old position behind.

One thing is certain: Allowing fear to rule your life is a definite way to hold yourself back from accomplishing all that you're destined to do. When we fear something, we give it power over us. In a sense, we become a magnet, drawing the fearful thing or situation toward us because we've thought so much about it and given it so much energy.

Write the word *fear* on a piece of paper. Do you see the word? Now take your pen or pencil and cross it out. It doesn't belong to you any longer and I pray it never will again.

In its place, write the word *faith.* Have faith in yourself and your abilities and faith in the Universe to provide what is best for you.

It's far better to know you've given something your best efforts than to think that fear kept you from even trying.

Affirmations:

1) *"I am bathed in the light of protection."*

2) *"A higher force is in charge. I relax and let good come forward. Let go, let God."*

3) *"I relax in the knowledge that I am never alone."*

4) *"I rejoice in my perfection. I have no room for fear or doubt."*

FINANCIAL PROBLEMS/PROSPERITY

It's a fact of life that everyone needs some form of financial stability to survive in the world. If you're not yet earning what you feel you should be earning, at least be grateful that you *are* earning something. Be content for the moment, but visualize yourself earning more, paying your bills, opening or adding to a savings account, making a down payment on a car, home or condo.

If you're offered a job that doesn't pay as much as you'd like and you've tried to get your employer to increase the salary, don't let pride get in the way of employment! Accept the best salary you've been offered and make plans to gain an increase as time moves on.

Most importantly: Do you enjoy your career? Love what you're doing and I firmly believe the money will follow. When you love your job it shows in the quality of work you produce, which in turn will eventually translate to an increase in salary.

If, however, you work in an office but secretly long to own your own business, make plans to open that business—otherwise, the eight hours you spend at work could seem like eighteen.

Of course, visualizing prosperity isn't limited to employment matters. You can apply the principles of prosperity to the sale of property or possessions, for example. So, if you have a home for sale, visualize the right buyer coming into your vibrations, someone who will love the home and take care of it as you have.

Don't hold onto the property, whatever it may be. Allow it to find another loving owner. In your mind, release the property. It has served its purpose for you. The affirmations to follow can work equally as well in a circumstance such as this, where your goal is to release an item on your way to acquiring something new that might be better suited to you.

Sweet Spirits, there's nothing wrong with wanting a lovely home, a nice car, and ample money in the bank. There's nothing wrong with wanting to be a millionaire, for that matter, if (and it's an important "if"), in return you're willing to contribute to your favorite charity. Giving money or help to those less fortunate is a way of giving thanks, of giving back to the Universe some of the blessings you've received.

The spirits and higher forces who helped you receive the financial blessings will indeed appreciate your gratitude, and often reward you yet again (though of course we don't *give* with that intention).

Affirmations:

1) *"I attract the abundance I seek. Financial contentment is mine."*

2) *"Health, happiness and prosperity are meant for me. I reach out and claim them as mine."*

3) *"All my needs are provided for. I am filled with joyful abundance."*

4) *"I attract the abundance I seek. Financial contentment is mine."*

5) *"The home that I seek, seeks me."*

FORGIVENESS (see also ANGER)

If you can't *forget*, you really can't *forgive*. But perhaps being more tolerant of a person or situation is the best approach to take. Try, try to forgive. It will benefit you eventually.

I've often told my clients that, as I see it, there are three sides to every argument: your opinion, the other person's opinion, and the *right* opinion. Let's put it this way: Disagreements are hardly ever black and white. The truth usually lies somewhere in the middle, without either person being totally right or wrong. Please, make this one of your philosophies: A true friend can never lose a friend.

But why hold any person or situation responsible for your anger or frustration? Anger only festers and makes you uncomfortable. It holds you back from true happiness, and you deserve to be happy. Being happy is yours for the asking.

Have you had a disagreement with someone? Forgiveness has to start somewhere, so why not let it begin with you? You'll feel so good about yourself.

I'm a firm believer in giving a person a second chance. The philosophy of "turning the other cheek" holds true for me. However, be fair to yourself as well. If you've turned the other cheek—in other words, if you've given someone the benefit of the doubt, and a second or even a third chance—and they show no signs of remorse over the hurt they may be causing you, then perhaps it is best to turn your energy elsewhere, to something or someone more constructive and positive.

Affirmations:

1) *"I release all unhappy memories. My destiny lies within me."*

2) *"The good I feel for others returns one hundredfold to me."*

3) *"I will learn from the past, but I will live in the future."*

4) *"My mind and heart are open to forgiveness."*

5) *"I forget painful memories and move on with my new life."*

GRIEF (see also LOVE, FINANCIAL PROBLEMS/PROSPERITY)

Grief is a very private affair. There are really no guidelines for the grieving process, and unless you've lived through it, there's no way to explain it. It is almost unbearable.

When we love someone with all our heart, and they pass on to the other side, part of the grief process involves feeling badly for ourselves. We truly long for the one who's passed, and we miss their contribution to our lives. We truly miss their being with us in the flesh, which of course is selfish on our behalf.

It's perfectly normal to cry because we miss someone, so please, don't hold back the tears. And there's certainly no time frame for grief. Some recover sooner than others and that's a very personal and individual matter. But I offer one word of caution: While it's true that tears are normal and to be expected, too many tears over too long a period of time tends to hold your dear loved one Earthbound.

Instead of their being free to release Earthly problems and concerns, they see you crying and are torn between two worlds. They'd like to move on to progress completely to the spirit world, but they love you and feel responsible for your unhappiness.

Dear ones, please understand, though, that as much as they might want to come back in the flesh to end your tears, they cannot. Their fate is to move on, to take their place in the spirit world. Only then will they be fully able to release all of their pain and suffering and of course you want that for them.

Releasing your loved one doesn't mean forgetting them. It only means you love them so much that you want what's meant for them and what's best for them. If our loved one had left us for a better job opportunity or for more schooling that took them away from us, we would be happy for them. In many ways, their passage into the spirit world should be looked upon in the same way. The passing of a loved one is meant to be a promotion, a graduation, a reward to them for a job well done, a life well lived.

And of course they can return to visit you in spirit once they've rested and adjusted to their new "life" in Paradise.

Affirmations:

1) *"My loved one is only a thought away."*

2) *"I release my loved one to a healthier, happier place."*

3) *"There is no loss, only change."*

4) *"I relax in the knowledge that I am never alone."*

5) *"There is a living force of strength within me."*

6) *"My pain grows weaker and I grow stronger."*

7) *"I forget painful memories and move on with my new life."*

HABITS (see also TEMPTATION)

"I'm an alcoholic." "I'm a smoker." "I'm a nail biter." "I'm fat because I eat too much." Whatever the habit, attaching a label to your unhealthy activity gives it strength. It becomes your identity and therefore has the potential for power over you. Your subconscious registers that label and accepts it as fact. Therefore, every time you say, "I'm a gambler" or whatever label your habit has, you're reinforcing the situation.

Naturally we must acknowledge that we have a problem, that we overindulge or possibly abuse a particular substance or activity. But once we acknowledge the problem ("Sometimes I drink too much," "I smoke more than I'd like to") we should move on toward correcting the problem. Habits *can* be broken, changes *can* be made, the power *is* within you, no question about it.

Here's a treasured secret I'll share with you. While you have to really *want* to quit a negative habit for your own good, sometimes the best way to give up a habit is to make a promise to a loved one on the other side. Promise your dear mother or brother, husband or wife that you'll do this in their memory, because you know they love you and want you to be healthy. Make a pact with this dear spirit and it may well be the secret key which keeps your resolve strong.

For example, you might speak out loud to that spirit, saying something like, "You were the best wife (or mother, etc.) anyone could ever want. I know all too well that you're not "dead," you've only passed on and are in the next room. I promise you, because I know it would please you, that I will never have another cigarette again." (Tailor this for whatever your habit might be.)

I suggest you keep this vow a very special secret between your loved one and yourself. We've no doubt all had the experience of telling our well-meaning Earthly friends that we're on a diet or we're giving up alcohol, only to have them say, "Oh, you can have just *one* drink . . . " or "You *have* to have a piece of cake!" In their own way, they're trying to be kind and hospitable, telling us not to be so strict with ourselves.

But when you've made up your mind to something, no one, not even a well-intentioned friend, should try to change your mind. So what's the easiest thing to do? Don't tell them to begin with! Instead of saying "I'm on a diet," say, "No, thank you, I just don't care for anything sweet right now."

The day will come, after the weight is off or you've truly stopped smoking and know you're beyond having the bad habit return, when you can share your success with everyone. In the meantime, while you're in the process of changing, why not keep the wonderful secret to yourself?

Now, if by some chance you *do* have some difficulty—if you fall and have that cigarette a few weeks or months later—know that it's unfortunate, but it could happen to anyone, no matter how strong his or her intentions might have been. Rather than harming yourself with too much self-criticism or blame, talk to that spirit again, saying something like, "I slipped and fell, but I'll try again, especially for you."

Know that this dear one in spirit is in a better position now than they ever were to help you and give you strength to overcome your habit. They love you and they'll love the fact that you're doing something to help yourself, which will also honor them.

And don't forget to make a promise to yourself as well. You are important. Tell yourself that you deserve to feel better and to look better. You deserve the positive results which can come from making a change in bad habits. Know that when the time is right, you will be released from your bad habit or behavior problem. Be prepared, do your best, then release your problem to whatever higher force you believe in.

Affirmations:

1) *"I learn to take charge of my life when I start to control my thoughts."*

2) *"I make peace with my body."*

3) *"My mind is gentle and harmonious. I break free from my need to _____."(habit)*

4) *"The power to change is mine."*

HEALTH

Tour any hospital and I guarantee you'll feel better about your own health problems. There's always someone who has problems worse than yours, and sometimes it takes an awakening to that fact to help you feel better about yourself.

Certainly health is a physical concern but it also involves a state of mind. Consider the following examples as proof that health is channeled through our brain. You're pruning roses and stand back to happily admire your handiwork. But when you do, you look down at a finger and see that it's bleeding. Ouch! Suddenly that finger (which felt perfectly fine before) stings, and it may even start to throb. Your mind has told you, "There's blood—it must be painful."

Or, you have a dreadful toothache. The pain just hasn't let up. Finally, you get a dentist appointment. And miraculously, your pain decreases. It may even disappear. In this case, your brain has registered the fact that "help is on the way," and that may be all that's necessary to bring some relief.

Of course there are bona fide illnesses. Some of them, unfortunately, are quite serious. In these cases, in addition to traditional medical help, many people are turning to spiritual healing and prayer.

If you are fortunate enough to receive a Divine healing, even in the form of some relief from your problem, by all means *accept* that healing. Don't question it. Accept it and be oh-so-grateful.

Many people are blessed with the ability to give a Divine healing. You can try this with family and friends: Rub your hands together and then hold your palms toward the person you're sending your healing energy to. Remember now that you don't send them your OWN energy, but instead energy that is circulating outside of you. Ask the spirit world to help energize you and direct healing toward the person. Visualize the person in total perfection, without pain or illness.

If the illness is within yourself, you can do the same exercise on yourself. You or the person you're sending the healing to may feel extremely warm, or there may be a tingling sensation throughout the body.

Can a healing always take place? It would be wrong to suggest that it can. There is always the chance for a miracle, but there are times when someone is not meant to be healed.

Their time may have come to move on to the spirit world, and if that's the case, it would be wrong of us to demand that they stay.

When I ask for a healing for myself or a loved one, I mention the health problem and ask that the situation be healed completely, but I close my meditation with a phrase which seems to say it all: "If it is Thy will."

Affirmations:

1) *"Health, happiness and prosperity are meant for me. I reach out and claim them as mine."*

2) *"My mind and body are in total perfection."*

3) *"I am perfect, whole, and complete. I love and approve of myself. I am free to be me."*

4) *"Every cell in my body is alive, keeping me happy and healthy."*

5) *"The white light of protection surrounds, soothes, and engulfs me."*

6) *"I am bathed in a healthy glow."*

7) *"My surgery is successful. My body is cleared of imperfections."*

8) *"My test results reflect the clear and total perfection of my body."*

LONELINESS

Loneliness doesn't necessarily have anything to do with being alone. You can feel lonely in a crowded room if the people you're surrounded by aren't really in tune with you.

If you're finding it difficult to carry on a meaningful conversation with a particular person or group of people, maybe it's because they're the wrong people for you. Are you a computer whiz? Are old movies your passion? Do sports activities occupy your thoughts and time? Whatever your interests, try seeking out people with those same interests, instead of trying to fit into an environment where you're uncomfortable. Attend a computer show, go to a baseball game, find a theatre showing classic films. You may find that you won't feel so alone, but instead will feel you're finally in your rightful place.

If you don't feel like being around people, stay at home. Reading a good book, watching a fascinating film on television, painting or doing some gardening can seem like a wonderful activity, with the perfect company—YOU!

Many people are alone by choice. They tell me "I'm very discriminating when it comes to companions or friends. Unless I can be with people I truly enjoy, I'm totally comfortable with myself."

One client of mine said she spent many nights at singles bars or dances, figuring that was a way many people met one another. "But I didn't like it," she said. "It was too noisy, too tense. I prefer the quiet peace of being alone, so I can clear my head."

Being content with oneself is an important goal, and it is the highest compliment you can pay to yourself. When you can say that you enjoy your own company, you are indeed saying a great deal.

However, in the meantime, if you truly feel you *must* meet someone, try to take a class, go to a museum, or volunteer your time for a worthy cause. Whether it's a potential love interest or a friend, you're bound to meet others who enjoy the same thing.

Affirmations:

1) *"Love surrounds and protects me. I have a special place in the Universe."*

2) *"I relax in the knowledge that I am never alone."*

3) *"I express love and attract happiness and companionship."*

4) *"The love that I seek seeks me."*

5) *"I draw loving friendship into my life."*

LOVE

Many years ago, I came up with the following definition of love: "Love is a passion that issues forth from the heart and exhilarates to all parts of the anatomy."

Love is a very basic emotion. We can't rationalize it, we can't explain why it happens between any two particular people.

But whether we can explain it or not, we know it exists, and it is the source of an abundance of joy, and unfortunately, sometimes pain, as well.

But psychically I know there are ways to enhance the joy and overcome or avoid the pain.

Too often, it appears that people expect instant love, the same way they expect instant coffee or drive-thru fast food. Having given psychic readings to many great names in entertainment, I'm always alerted to people who come up to me after a lecture and say, "I want to be a star, but I moved to Hollywood two months ago and nothing's happened yet!"

Dear Ones, no one greets you with a sign saying, "Welcome to Hollywood—here's a film contract." It takes talent, patience and hard work.

Love must be dealt with in the same way. No one is going to approach you with a sign saying, "I'd like to be your boyfriend," or "Here I am—I'm your new girlfriend."

No matter how romantic-minded we are, the reality is that love takes time and effort.

When you *do* have a date, give a relationship a chance to build from it rather than expecting a relationship to be established after just one dinner or movie.

Are you dating someone and feel you might be in love but you're doubting your feelings? Perhaps you're wondering whether this person is right for you. If you've said to yourself, "He's too young for me," or "We're too different from one another to have a romance," remember that love knows no boundaries. Love sees no differences, no sexual preferences. Trust your feelings; trust your instincts. Of course while we're talking about the aspects of love, this also means that if you have a deep, instinctive feeling that something is seriously wrong in your relationship, in the sense that your partner is abusive or putting one or both of you in real danger, listen to *that* feeling, as well.

Is this the second or third time a marriage or relationship has ended for you? It may be time to do some soul searching, or perhaps it's time to look subjectively in the mirror.

If your relationships repeatedly end, you may be finding the same type of person over and over again and he or she may be the wrong *type* of person for you. I know it might seem too analytical where love is concerned, but for a moment, think of the qualities or traits that attracted you to each person you've been involved with. Then think of what, in your opinion, went wrong in the relationship. Did a personality trait become annoying or overpowering? Finally, consider what you really need from a relationship and what you feel you can provide in return. This evaluation might give real insight into yourself and your relationship.

Now, is there something you feel you can improve upon? Is it your temper, a tendency toward sarcasm, or perhaps being too hard to please? If so, accept the blame (for perhaps a few moments at least!) if you feel you sincerely deserve a share of the blame. And as you know, in most cases, both parties are to blame to some degree. Most importantly, work at improving the trait you feel may have contributed to your relationship problem, and then move on.

Persistent and violent arguments could definitely mean you should re-evaluate a relationship. But don't be so quick to break up a romance because of a simple disagreement. If you feel your partner isn't giving enough time to the relationship, talk things through rather than abandoning what might otherwise be a good romance. Your partner may not be aware that there *is* a problem until you share your feelings and bring the problems out into the open. And be willing to take some share of the responsibility for the situation, especially if you do seem to enter into and then end one relationship after another.

What are good criteria for determining whether a relationship is worth saving? Ask yourself whether you'd stay with the person you're involved with if someone else came along instead. If not, you may just be "in love with love," holding on to *anyone*, rather than being alone.

But being without a romance needn't be negative. Give yourself the luxury of being very selfish for a bit of time—enjoy the breathing space you've been given. Perhaps you need the time for yourself to fix your home, visit the doctor for a physical check-up you've been putting off, or to spend more time with friends you've been telling you'll get together with "soon."

You can use the time to take a class you've thought about or to begin a hobby you've wanted to explore. You might be surprised. Though you should take the class or begin the hobby because you want to do it for YOU, while you're busy with your new endeavor, love just might come along when you least expect it.

Many people seem to be in search of their soul mate, and it's a wonderful goal. Soul mates are best friends. They knew each other in a past life and have found one another again in *this* life. Soul mates are able to complete one another's thoughts, and they can hold one another's hands without touching. True soul mates know each other's wants and can communicate with adoring eyes of love, even across a crowded room.

We may recognize a soul mate instantaneously because the bond may be that strong. But consider this possibility: You may be *with* your soul mate and not realize it. Again, there'll be no sign held by your romantic partner saying, "I'm your soul mate." Even those who on the surface don't seem to be ideally suited may, in reality, be soul mates. Re-evaluate your relationship. Look at the strong points, the level of communication, comfort, and pleasure. If your two hearts beat as one, you have this special bond we call soul mates.

Do we all find that all-encompassing, overwhelming love called a soul mate? Possibly not. There may be other plans for us where love is concerned.

But please, Sweet Spirits, don't discount fun or romance which may come your way. It would be a shame to turn your back on love while searching for something that at the moment is not in the Universe's plans for you.

Live, love, laugh, and enjoy yourselves!

Affirmations:

1) *"The love that I seek, seeks me."*

2) *"The love that I give returns to bless me."*

3) *"My heart heals, my tears dry, I prepare to love again."*

4) *"Love surrounds and protects me. I have a special place in the Universe."*

5) *"I am filled with the pure light of love."*

6) *"I relax in the knowledge that I am never alone."*

7) *"My anger is soothed, my pain is healed, I attract love again."*

NEGATIVITY

Expect negativity and you won't be disappointed. Focus on negativity and it's sure to come your way.

The next time you're feeling negative about something, try turning it around, looking for the possible good. Your date called to cancel? Maybe you would have been in an accident if you'd gone. You've waited all week to play golf, but wake up Saturday morning and it's pouring rain? Perhaps there's a good reason for the delay in your plans. What a perfect opportunity to catch up on reading or spend time with your family, or maybe even do something around the house they'll thank you for later.

Sweet Spirits, don't expect something monumental to happen all the time. Sometimes the best we can hope for is a simple day of work, or a non-eventful but relaxing day of rest. Don't become discouraged if some days pass quietly by. If you doubt that goodness is coming, you will keep it away. We are a magnet for good or evil in our lives. The good may already be at work. Look for it, but also trust in it even if it's momentarily hard to find.

If feeling negative becomes a habit, look for something simple that might lie behind the problem. Are you sleeping enough? If not, take what I call "kittywinks"—a mini version of a "cat nap"—in other words, just a few refreshing minutes of rest.

Whether you're a man or a woman, you deserve to pamper yourself. Do something nice for yourself and see if you don't automatically feel better about the people and things around you.

Affirmations:

1) *"No negative vibrations will enter, now or ever."*

2) *"I attract only good in my life."*

3) *"Each day I prepare for a better tomorrow."*

4) *"I refuse to accept a negative thought. It doesn't belong to me."*

PEACE OF MIND/PROTECTION

Peace of mind cannot be bought; no such price tag exists. Though we may make purchases to help us achieve peace of mind or relaxation, we cannot buy peace, per se. Peace comes from within. But peace and contentment are also hard to recognize, and sometimes we have more of these precious commodities than we think.

Sit with a hot cup of coffee or tea, or a refreshingly cool glass of water or soda, and briefly review your life. Are you in reasonably good health? That's something that should give you pleasure. Are you surrounded by family members who love you? That's certainly a bonus in life. Do you have a pet you enjoy, who looks at you adoringly? The list goes on: flowers, paintings, good books, music, even something as simple as a hot cup of coffee on a cold morning, or the way you feel rested and invigorated after a good night's sleep. Simplicity can give you peace of mind; it needn't come only from major events or possessions.

So many of you believe as I do, in the spirit world. If you are one of these people, know that our loved ones in spirit—our guardian angels and protectors—are watching over us and helping us in all aspects of our lives. That certainly should give us peace of mind.

Looking at your life, reviewing it in this way, and seeing not what you lack but what you are and what you have, may make you realize you have more to make you happy than you previously believed.

You have it within you to achieve so much more, if you desire it. As the old saying goes, "Where there's a will, there's a way."

May I also suggest, Sweet Spirits, that it's very noble indeed to work or pray for peace in the world. Naturally we all want this to be a reality. But we can best achieve that goal by first achieving peace within ourselves. Strive to feel secure, try to be content. Become the best "you" possible, and then that strong person, that peaceful person, can better serve mankind.

Affirmations:

1) *"My mind and body are in total perfection."*

2) *"I am perfect, whole, and complete. I love and approve of myself. I am free to be me."*

3) *"I relax, release, and let go."*

SLEEP

It was always a tradition in my house as I was growing up to never go to bed angry with someone, or thinking of what might have been. I've tried to keep that philosophy to this day.

If there's something I want to accomplish but haven't been able to do on a particular day, I tell myself, "It's too late to do anything about it tonight. Let it go. Get a good night's sleep and you'll be fresh to start work again in the morning." It works for me.

Surprisingly, many things that seem bothersome at bedtime seem less important in the morning, anyway. The distance of sleep puts things in a different perspective.

Not everyone needs eight hours' sleep. For some people five hours are as refreshing as ten. Even if you don't immediately fall asleep when you lie down, you're resting your eyes and body, you're relaxing your mind. Allow yourself the luxury of relaxing. Release your thoughts to the night and float away. Relax, release, and let go.

I invite you to try a technique I often use to prepare myself for sleep. Lying in bed, I say, "Every nerve, every cell, every muscle, every organ in my body is soothed and protected. Relaxation begins at the top of my head. I leave behind any thoughts or worries. My neck and shoulders release any tension. My arms and hands are relaxed. Peace and protection flow through my central nervous system, through my digestive system, through my spinal column, through my back, hips, legs, and feet. I am bathed in peace and contentment and I know I am free to float off to sleep. I've done all that I can for today and I deserve this beautiful time for serenity and relaxation."

Affirmations:

1) *"I release all tension and drift on peaceful waves of contentment."*

2) *"I allow myself to relax; I deserve this special time of rest."*

3) *"My mind and body are in total perfection. I relax, release, and let go."*

STRESS

Stress has such a negative connotation. It has become one of the most used, and in my opinion *overused,* words in our vocabulary.

Yet there is such a thing as *good* stress. It gets your adrenaline pumping, it gives you the strength or courage you need and the energy necessary to get things done. Tap into that good stress and make it work for you. This works for me and for many of my clients and friends.

Of course you can have too much stress in your life, in which case meditation or relaxation techniques like those I suggest in my cassette tapes "10 Steps to a Better You" and "Learn from the Past . . . Live in the Future" may help. I'll also suggest some relaxing thoughts at the end of this book.

Does stress kill? If you ask me, if stress were directly responsible for passing away, you wouldn't be able to walk over all the bodies! Most people can learn to manage their stress or to accept the fact that it can act as a spring-board for good. It can be a source of powerful energy if you work *through* it instead of giving *in to* it.

I had a wonderful telephone conversation one day with a friend of mine, who told me one of her favorite sayings pertaining to stress. "Don't lie in bed worrying about your problems," she said. "Get up, get going, work on your problems. God won't hit a moving target!" Of course this is a delightfully witty observation, but it's also incredibly true, and I invite you to think about it the next time you feel stress has invaded your life.

Perhaps the best way to counteract stress is by taking action. Instead of becoming irritated or agitated about all the things you have to do before guests arrive for a party you're hosting, for example, get up, get moving. *Do* something about even one of the things that worry you.

Affirmations:

1) *"I relax, release, and let go."*

2) *"Nothing and no one disturbs me. I am wrapped in a safe cocoon."*

3) *"My mind is gentle and harmonious. I am free to be me."*

4) *"The pure light of love surrounds me."*

5) *"No negative vibrations will enter, now or ever."*

6) *"I am fulfilling my purpose in life. The Universe is revealing its plan for me."*

7) *"There is nothing so powerful that I cannot bear it."*

8) *"Trial periods are proof that God cares."*

TEMPTATION (see also HABITS)

I encourage you to read the segment on habits because temptation is often what drives us to develop a bad habit.

But temptation is also a topic in its own right, because we are tempted to do things that are not good for us or that have negative impact on our lives. These temptations have little to do with bad habits; they are instead negative actions.

Four areas of temptation seem to be most prominent, judging by the clients I see privately. These areas appear to cause the most harmful effects on our lives: food, sex, work, and lies.

Temptation for Food

Overindulging in food (or in the reverse, not eating enough) can be a major problem. If you feel your overeating has caused you to gain weight, I encourage you to never use the word "fat", but instead to say perhaps "pleasingly plump." The very word "fat" has a negative connotation to it.

Issues regarding food abuse may be among the hardest to resolve. We can live without alcohol or cigarettes. We can exist if we give them up, even for a few hours at a time or one day at a time.

But we are confronted with the need for food at least three times a day. There's simply no way to avoid the need each time mealtime comes around. For this reason, even a small step in the right direction toward proper weight management should be seen as success in your mind. If you plan to lose some weight, set reasonable goals. Every time you pass up dessert, reward yourself with a healthy alternative you enjoy—a book, a movie, a new CD.

I will leave it to you to debate the old adage of whether it's possible to be "too rich," but common sense tells us you can *certainly* be "too thin."

Weight is a personal matter and no one can or should tell you what, precisely, you should weigh. But moderation is the key. One thing I'm sure everyone would agree on is that you *can't* be too healthy. So let health be your guideline, be honest with yourself. If you find that you feel uncomfortable with your weight, don't deny it. If you're short-winded, if you can't move the way you used to, if you don't have the strength you once had, or perhaps if you don't have the sparkle in your eyes you once saw in the mirror, your body may be talking to you and asking you for help. Be good to yourself, and vow to look good for your own satisfaction, not because you want the world to see you in a certain way.

Rather than attempting to look like someone else—someone perhaps impossibly thin—strive instead to look like the best (and healthiest) *you* possible.

Temptation for Sex

I preface this section by saying that I'm no prude. I believe that sex can be a wonderful source of expression and pleasure. However from time to time, I've had clients tell me they use sex as a 'weapon' in a sense ("If my husband/wife won't do what I want, I'll withhold sex from him/her"). Most of us realize that this is not good. Sex wasn't intended to be used *against* another human being. It was meant to be enjoyed *with* another human being.

I've also encountered very young clients, females in particular, who feel sex is a "must." They feel they have to be intimate with their boyfriend or they'll lose him. Dear ones, if sex is all that's keeping the relationship alive, then what are you losing? Where is the companionship, the laughter, the mutual interests and support?

Still others approach me for counseling because they feel addicted to sex. Sex is the only way they feel they can gain approval or affection. I tell them, as I tell you, that sex is not your identity. You are a worthwhile person. You have personality traits or talents that make you special. Find and cultivate those aspects of your life and then incorporate sexual relations into your life when, and with whom, you choose, because you want to, not because they make you feel like "someone." You ARE someone already!

Temptation for Overworking

Ambition is wonderful. Striving for success is admirable. Rising to the top in your field of work is something many people hope to achieve. Naturally, reaching a high level of success often takes hard work and long hours. I've always thought it odd that someone would object to their mate's hard work, knowing they were doing it for the good of the family, to provide a pleasant lifestyle, and a nice home.

But there is a fine line between working hard and *overworking*, becoming obsessed with business to the exclusion of family or friends. There comes a point when we may have to evaluate, "Is this work necessary to do right now, or could I play ball with my son or go shopping with my daughter? Which would truly benefit us more?" Some people hide in their work, too, it seems, avoiding the realities of a family or social life.

Temptation for Lies

Does a "little white lie" hurt? Perhaps not. In fact, perhaps there are occasions when it is actually appropriate, in order to avoid hurting someone's feelings. But beware stretching or embellishing upon the truth, Sweet Spirits! I've always thought it would take too much effort and too perfect a memory to keep track of lies told, when the simple truth is so much easier!

Whenever someone tells me, "I'm leaving my boyfriend because someone told me he was cheating on me," I say,

"Why not ask your boyfriend directly? Go to the *source*, instead of settling for rumors."

Remember, too, that every story has an author. So if someone says to you, "I heard something unkind about you today," insist the person tell you what they heard and from whom. Then confront that person directly. If untruths or unkind words are being said, you deserve to know all the facts.

Affirmations:

1) *"I make peace with my body."*

2) *"All that I eat turns to beauty and health."*

3) *"I control my body; I control what I eat."*

4) *"My body and I work together toward perfection."*

5) *"I am perfect, whole, and complete. I love and approve of myself. I am free to be me."*

6) *"I seek the truth; I speak the truth."*

7) *"I deserve relaxation. I reward my hard work."*

Dear Sweet Spirits, I ask you to please avail yourself of these affirmations. Visualize your way to the happiness, strength, and prosperity you desire. When you awaken each day, expect the best from the day. Expect it and you can receive it.

Start each day singing, if you're so inclined. However, do so after breakfast, if you believe as I do in the old adage, "Sing before breakfast and you'll cry before dinner"!

Believe that your mind and body are energized and refreshed when you awaken. I invite you to try this energizing exercise. Place your hands near one another, palms facing each other and only the fingers touching, forming a pyramid shape. If you can, you may want to remove your shoes and assume relatively the same position with your feet. Visualize electricity flowing through you. This "locks in" your energy, recharging you spiritually and personally.

At the end of your day, reverse the visualization, seeing yourself relaxed, peaceful and calm. Do your best at all times, and then rest in the knowledge that you've done all you can for the day. Slowly and softly, speaking only to yourself, repeat this most powerful and endearing of all affirmations: "The past is the past and the charm of the past is that it is the past." Remember, you are putting aside any painful or guilt-ridden memories. You are letting go of anything that disturbs you and you can awaken to a fresh start.

Accept only positive vibrations. One of my favorite sayings is by St. Francis de Salle, and it's carved into a plaque outside a church I attend frequently. I offer it to you as a marvelous way of ridding yourself of your concerns for the day. Regardless of your religion, I feel psychically that you'll find great comfort in it:

"The same everlasting Father who cares for you today will care for you tomorrow and every day. Either he will shield you from suffering, or give you unfailing strength to bear it.

"Be at peace, then, and put aside all anxious thoughts and imaginations."

You deserve all the good you are longing for, Sweet Spirits, and starting today—right now—you are making your goals a reality.

-MY FAVORITE AFFIRMATIONS-

—MY FAVORITE AFFIRMATIONS—

—MY FAVORITE AFFIRMATIONS—

—MY FAVORITE AFFIRMATIONS—

—MY FAVORITE AFFIRMATIONS—